Pet Rabbits

Cecelia H. Brannon

Enslow Publishing
101 W. 23rd Street
Suite 240
New York, NY 10011
USA

enslow.com

Published in 2017 by Enslow Publishing, LLC.
101 W. 23rd Street, Suite 240, New York, NY 10011

Library of Congress Cataloging-in-Publication Data

Names: Brannon, Cecelia H., author.
Title: Pet rabbits / Cecelia H. Brannon.
Description: New York, NY : Enslow Publishing, 2017. | Series: All about pets | Audience: Age 4-up. |
  Audience: Pre-school, excluding K. | Includes bibliographical references and index.
Identifiers: LCCN 2015045458| ISBN 9780766076051 (library bound) | ISBN 9780766076303 (pbk.) |
  ISBN 9780766075870 (6-pack)
Subjects: LCSH: Rabbits--Juvenile literature.
Classification: LCC SF453.2 .B73 2017 | DDC 636.932/2--dc23
LC record available at http://lccn.loc.gov/2015045458

Printed in Malaysia

To Our Readers: We have done our best to make sure all website addresses in this book were active and appropriate when we went to press. However, the author and the publisher have no control over and assume no liability for the material available on those websites or on any websites they may link to. Any comments or suggestions can be sent by e-mail to customerservice@enslow.com.

Photos Credits: Cover, Topmasterchief/Shutterstock.com; p. 1 gabczi/Shutterstock.com; pp. 3 (left), 4–5 ThorMitty/Shutterstock.com; pp. 3 (center), 14 Hirohito Takada/Shutterstock.com; pp. 3 (right), 16 Rocketclips, Inc./Shutterstock.com; p. 6 Viorel Sima/Shutterstock.com; p. 8 bikeriderlondon/Shutterstock.com; p. 10 Darren Baker/Shutterstock.com; p. 12 dsom/Shutterstock.com; p. 18 Russamee/Shutterstock.com; p. 20 T. M. McCarthy/Shutterstock.com; p. 22 Surkov Dimitri/Shutterstock.com.

Contents

Words to Know

cage

vegetables

veterinarian

3

Rabbits live in large cages. They can be inside or outside!

Rabbits have long, soft ears. Some rabbits have ears that stand up. Other rabbits have ears that hang down.

Rabbits have very soft fur that is fun to pet. You can hold your rabbit, too!

Rabbits come in many colors. Some are brown, black, gray, or white. Some are more than one color!

Rabbits need fresh air and room to run and hop. This helps them stay healthy.

Rabbits eat fruits and vegetables such as lettuce, apples, and carrots. They also have special food called pellets.

An animal doctor is called a veterinarian (vet). A vet can keep your rabbit healthy.

Some rabbits are shy and do not like to be around people. Talking to rabbits softly can help.

Never catch rabbits from the wild and bring them home. They do not make good pets.

Rabbits make great pets! Take good care of your rabbit.

Read More

Ganeri, Anita. *Bunny's Guide to Caring for Your Rabbit.* Portsmouth, NH: Heinemann, 2013.

Heneghan, Judith. *Love Your Rabbit.* New York: Windmill Books, 2013

Websites

Science Kids
>   sciencekids.co.nz/sciencefacts/animals/rabbit.html

Enchanted Learning
>   enchantedlearning.com/subjects/mammals/farm/Rabbitprintout
>   .shtml

Index

Guided Reading Level: B
Guided Reading Leveling System is based on the guidelines recommended by Fountas and Pinnell.

Word Count: 156